Adam before His Mirror

Also by Ned O'Gorman · The Night of the Hammer

Adam

before

His

Mirror

by Ned O'Gorman

Harcourt,

Brace &

World, Inc.

New York

4/1961
Genl.

To Sarah Moss Lorimer

and Jeremiah K. Durick

Contents

Adam before His Mirror

The Day the Steuben Glass Building Breaks

We shall all be gashed terribly
in that season of thermal shock
when prisms flail the light and dark
stings of glass point
toward the sun.

Tumblers, tureens, crystal plums,
vast jugs of mica, cups
and tankards, candelabra, pots
of steaming glacial heat
will fall like honed feathers

on our heads. The vitric turret
splinters, cut-glass flowers
bloom in the blood. The hours
ring in high C
as millefiori crosshatch

the chest. The lamb in
blazon mirror shatters
in an optic blaze. The axis fractures
and this O crystal world
buckles and glass

bends upon glass.
It was bound to go; too much
human breath in those rooms; truss
and spiritus explode
after long curing.

On the edge of the cornice
hanging by its teeth
a glass unicorn in a brief
gambit before harrowing
points into the blue heaven

and in a Venetian leap
lands like a leaf on the roof,
flashes the sun and stamps its hoof
that sends the shaft
plummeting toward the center.

Toward a Language of the Ineffable

The mind reigns in its ruddy element.
I have it, from superb messengers, that God
moves on the axis of light that lies between
the eyes and the golden center of the brain.
I know only the coign in the mind
where some face or thigh or song, in the black act
of thought, hammers through the sun;
but I dream of tongues for the fire in my dreams
and of the lovely yellow and blue flowers
that swarm on the honey-heights where his very step
is on the air and his palm presses downward
on the leaf; where his voice neighs and crushes
in my ears. I think of what the mind knows
and what the poem confines; how the infinite
seizes rhetoric and how the poem broods.
I pace the day, level with the light,
understanding nothing but the continual rush of beauty
that undoes custom and heralds ritual through me like blossoms.

3

The Tree House

All starts in the the air where the first
element of the world and place
of illuminations, in the fracture
of its fire, through the roots of the sea,
brings to this household on a cliff

the branches of the sun. Light
crackles in the hive of space, and beauty
holds a crystal to the mind, in this
hippodrome of winds, on this
wooded belvedere.

(But remember the mind at its thermal
joint where the eyes meet the sun
in a coincidence of two heats and cast
a dark cope on the stumbling frog
before your boys pin his brain,

burning as this sun burns.) O cousins
who live in the crag of the sun,
on a precipice of flowers, the center
leaps beneath you where roebuck
and birds in galleries of leaves

bring the world to odds. Bank
the northern slope with roses. Set up
the marble frieze of wild violets and scrolls
upon the light and watch the doric birch pierce
your dreams and the hill ride mightily and flower.

4
Poem

I often think of this: how grand the world was
before the poets made it over according
to their will. I look to see if I can find
the unreported, monolithic mind—
I think, and following my thought I find
that Troy was possible and Homer blind.

5
I Am a Falcon, Hooded . . .

I am a falcon, hooded, on God's wrist;
my talons hum with the blood of time
and in his greatcoat, belted with a twist
of mail, the falconer in the brine
of harvest stands amid battalions
of the sun, pulling a thread of light.
In leather hood, I hear their stallions,
stomping on the dirt but cannot move, my night
and day so locked and knotted in his will.
I am might, far more than the aerial prow
that breaks through the crust of the wind; my bill
can slam, maul, sunder, force and drill; on my brow
flash the studs and flags of the mind; my ruff
spills light. I am Aeronaut and know the sky;
I am towering animal and sonic beast; I am stuff
of butchery, brim with holocaust; I am the spy
of the ethers, but on God's wrist I am lead;
a feathered spume, brought like a wild,
naked feral boy to race the dead
in the white stadia of the moon. I am mild
pigeon in a cage of hide and though God's vein
beats through my claws, my head in black
obeisance pushes against a leathern pain.
I have murky thoughts and crack
ideas against the paragon. There is no attention
like this attention on the wrist
of beauty, gripping the holy hand, invention
urging the heart to unheard-of skills. I jog. I twist
as fires spring at his head and water grinds
the mortar and ichor of my frame. I hold—
and fly in being still. I see the hind
in the spinning field, the hill kicks under me, cold
flowers yield about my eyes. The falconer spoke
and his belt of mail cracks the air like a thunderbolt.

6

Reading Dante with Ionians

We did him, boys, with no care,
mucking through all that light
with our boots unlaced, right
into the face of God. We learned
the rhetoric of hell
and watched the celestial
flower wagon standing in the sun.

O my boys. All those things:
the sweet style of the world and
the unmaking of the mind; the land
of milk and honey, of roaring
kennels and lovers come to love
like cranes hovering above
a burning barn, pushed from nests

into the kinetic blast; the land
lying like a pulley between heaven
and hell, the leaven
of the sun and the racket of seraph.
We cannot tell how much we said,
how near we got to the head
and husk of the sanctified, but we

tried, O boys how we did try and never,
no matter if we're priest
or sybarite, husband or the least
dandy in the world's garden, will we know
again the bowl of heaven where the flow
and stammer of the Lord pitched
on the mind, how from this poem we learned

the possibilities of praise.

On Silence

Silence is the pulling in of nets
on the sand. It is a tent
in a square. Silence is the covenant
of noise when the mind sleeps
in its neutral passion.

It is the bulb of a tulip
since silence locks in variety
and antecedes spring. Silence
rises to the high places
of the heart where meadows

flower and the dark passages
reach into light.
It is the power of a drum.
The interval of silence
is like a coiled rope.

In man an antiphon sleeps
facing the sun, bound foursquare
by a golden cord. Silence
is the desolation of the cord
and the waking of the antiphon.

7
What's the Mind in the Argument

What's the mind in the argument
that brings down your hand so hard upon the table?
Is it the periods in light?
Is it the startling and crimson birds that descend
when idea of this kind follows idea of that kind
and then the resurrection of the blind?

What's the mind in the argument
that brings your foot down so hard upon the floor?
Is it the flutes and the marching?
Or the mind in its spells?
Is the apple flowering and the wild pear tree
or has the sun breathed in the sea?

What's the mind in the argument
that turns your head so fast upon the light?
Is it the frieze in the summer air?
Is it the skull, lustrous, on the sill?
When the heart and wild soul meet
the bird of morning the bird of evening greets.

What's the mind in the argument
that makes you wrap yourself in tawny shrouds?
Is it the thought of marvels that astound—
the tests of intellectual high deeds?
When the brain contrives against the walls of time,
begins the holy molestation of this rhyme.

9
Epithalamion

Bastioned with light, dear body and brave heart
mark with their exquisite and entire shadow
the sun and the suppliant dark. The steaming street,
bawdy waters and the summer fields hawk
the abundant season. The mind claims the heart's
bounty; the fire is intellectual, the ore, the vein.
Streams, in fluid saraband, move on floors of
hammered scales; from the blue parapet falls
the chrism of the sun like a hood of pitch
from a monstrance. Marked with signs of the wood,
a Unicorn, feet tangled with vine, harebells and crystal
studded on his horn, breaks through the
ramparts of the wilderness and from the grass rises
an ivory fence, cut with panes of gold and
dark magnificence, cap-a-pied the light.
And as candles, carried from dark temples
into the precincts of the night, bells, rivers, rocks,
cornices of grape, steeples and hills, conclude
the day. This is the spoil of silence,
and the Creatures, in radiant progress, flee into the hills.

A Reflection on a Picnic at Mount Savior
for Annette O'Gorman, Who Told Me First
about the Mountain Laurel

From God's completed mind man came intricate
as vineyards; from a will that had no other
passion but its own, man came real
as vegetables and willed catastrophes
and the fancies of lovers. The intellect
that spanned the circle and created it
built the bee his hexagon but no bevel ever
measured the mind's pitch or the will's connivance.

God the prowler, man the bait,
and Kevin mixed sardines and berries
on his plate.

I have been trained by nuns to think of God
all day and in extremes of passion
I find him in unlikely things; in seraphim
and soldiery, in the nadir and zenith
of gardens, in locked chests in the open sea,
in the moving lamentation of trumpets;
these differentiated things
seem to me God's wild mirrors.

Man's glory is his sweet eminence of intellect
that is the paradigm of all unlikely things;
the light at the summit of a hill;
how the baboon dares be baboon; the mountain laurel's
concave, stress and filigree. The shape of the world
is the infinite things it holds, as the arctic
holds the cleaved schooner, or the hand holds
the sea's salt, kelp, shell and indestructible green glass.

This Irishman moved with the desperate balance
of his race and in the silence of this holy place
he bent his eyes, like a hunter, to the ground
as if God peered from the turf,
rode on the turtle's back, smoldered
in the daisy's golden center or blazed
with the light on the tops of streams. In the
symmetry of praise, in a quiet thought stood

God the prowler, man the bait,
and Kevin mixed sardines and berries
on his plate.

A Poem in a Time of Deepest Pondering

There are dreams in my intellect's riding,
stupendous ponderings, that roll through
my mind as mountains roll through
the bucking light.

In the prance of my intellect's riding
a poem breaks through my mind
as a trout breaks through
the cords of midsummer.

The horns and bells of the earth's music
strike through the governance of suns
as cords of water shine in the bucking light
high on the plains of my intellect's riding.

To the Poet Who Concurred in Dragons

Dear Frank, when my mind blazes at its center
and the sun is the rack I lie on and the sea
the whole dream in my sleeping, I think of the
scene at Dornoch's firth I saw one day
riding down from Wick. The hours moved to dusk
and from the horned dark the sea broke through
my discontent and unhinged the runner
in the light who paced his track
like a tiger pacing the small Asia
of his cage. He leaped into my skin
and through the windowpane we crashed
the heather scattering in a raven squall
and on to the end of the firth's black
strand we ran hand in hand turning cart-
wheels in the jet air, splitting
the strata of the faithless sun to find
the center, one cosmos surveying another;
pushing through the water, as come to life
suddenly, a complete monster of the sea,
a dinosaur, brilliant, original, green, head high
in the clouds of my terror, shaking off
the sea animals that rested like a chain
of suns on his back. O I howled in my
own way, rearing up, daring the house of his
brain to open and receive me breakfast-food
or Isaac. And he walked through me clattering
his massive arms, slate eyes, blinking in
the sun and as I brought my hand up to my
mouth to stop a shriek that would have
pierced the center I saw the runner leave
my hand and with a leap so high and quick
I thought I was witness to a hanging he
mounted on the back of that rage of beast
and left me in my track, a wild lad
with a stone in my hand, disappearing
in the black waters, his head flashing
and my runner like a comet riding the waves.

Five Poems to Five Ladies

I   TO THE JEWESS

There is a stance of the mind
before burning: think of crackling salt
and Lot's beauty on the sizzling plain: the hind
in a holocaust: Moses halt
as crystal on the roaring bush.

II   TO THE GARDENER

Gardens are the earth's prism,
the exterior of the pith
at the center of the world; the chrism
in the air and the rift
in the seed at the flare of the rose.

III   TO THE ACTRESS

Think of the tragic harrowing: how the hour
heckled, how furies, one, two, three, filed
past the door. I know a power
beyond all contrition who smiled
and sprung the beams on the temple roof.

IV   TO THE POET

Sing of the green cycle from
idea to music to myth.
Sing of intellect and the thrum
at the center of thought: of the cliff
where the Logos backs into the deep.

V   TO THE HELPER

Eileen called bright cloth of red
to her employ—a fiery conceit
that summoned sparks and said
great things of passion—as a fleet
needle of fire through the wind.

Paolo Learns Gravity at Twelve O'Clock Noon

In the high noon, rocks
it in the air; reels
it through the air;
dredges up the gold
in it; scatters the tribes.
It raises the sun on end;
inches its way through
the foot and knocks
the knees; it apes
the lever; leans out over
the lips of gargoyles;
it nets the lark,
pulls over backward
the head; drowns the
army. It is centrifugal
to virgins; boys trip
on its edge. It hooks
its claws on the hip
and unlocks the turbulence
in rivers; rips up
the rivers and looses
them on the land;
screws down the lids
of kettles; explodes them.
Boom of it scours through
the night; holds up the dream;
dashes it down;
the dream settles and then
breaks through the limbs
to sever the ichor from
the vein. It spins tops;
tops go awry and burn swathes
through wheat; into the brace
of it all things are bent and
in the mortar of light both
intellect and light are crushed.

Two Visions

I

It was the last vision but one
(as I remember it) at seven
in the morning, standing in the light
of the window I had opened
on the rain. Though it was no vision
then, being early and just from bed,
naked as grass,
a coppered charioteer
with the loam of the sun on his eyes,
it began then, in that light—
thrashing in my ears.

When I walked down the steps
the rain had stopped, the sun
grew on the façade and ivy.
I had an incredible illusion:
Ezechiel, my stallion, bucked on the waters,
the street tipped toward the sun
and the oaken thill drove in
my chest as if a dryad
set her hatchet to the axletree and fell
the wagon, splintered, roots in air
on my heart.

II

There was Taintor's hill and then beyond it night.
The spell a boy carries in his will, a bright
vine in his crystal blood, sped through him
like a kite to the brim
of thought where all day dark trees bent
in the windows and bandits pitched a tent,
pennoned, on the hill. I loved him
and found his love uncommon. On the pond the wind
brought him on his way and standing there I watched
his eyes, and migratory birds red, yellow and black
sudden and imperial, broke into a sea of flowers at my back,
and winter, a white barge, boating through the dark
settled in the slivered air its cedar keel. A lark
of bandits had done enchantment on his world,
and like dynamos, from the frozen garden, whirled
a flight of new chimeras chittering in the sun.
I knew it was concluded; this was the center. I was undone.

Adam before His Mirror

You are my glove and waistcoat,
my boot and diamond pin,
my starched and pleated blouse;
my anchored collar, my scarf
and woven stocking. You are
the buckle on my hip,
my lacquered heel, my mask
for bees. You are my alb,
my amice and my hood, my walking
stick. You are my lute and drum,
my arbor and my bell, my rain
and sun, my season and my zoo.
You are circle of my hoop,
my scissor and my loom, my junction
and meadow, my sign, my darkness
and my light. You are hyssop
and mint, my crown, my hurdle.
You are the stillness
and the moving in my brain.
You are the span and fathom
of my chest. You are the arch
and vaulting of my skull. You are
root of my hand and exultation
in my reins. You are my image.
I am the stress and raiment of clay.

A Poem to Paula and a Poem to Ned

I

I have no thought but one, hot Paula
said. She has the mind of a siege!
The hands of untamed lioness. For her
I left the barricade! Ha! Breathe
on me sweet agate-eyes, fix me on
the sheet like a parenthesis. I have read
books on fire and know the down
and up of the heart and the regions of bed.
Believe me, small face (I left the burning
ship for thee), I've learned marriages and am learning.

II

The sun reigns. On the hilt of day
seraphs and troops of derring-do
punt through the waters. Wild Ned
climbs the flowering vine. The sun
strips him; he is all flaring;
the stripling of the river,
the fire-eater, all the patience of men
endured, now, so high, such a bird,
admits unto his thought the sphere of summer.
The vine grapples the summit of heaven
and the fruit of the vine is an absolute yellow orb.

A Hot Sunday

Once on a molten sabbath
rage brought down its hail
upon your head and you chattered
like a witch on the lip of hob.

You became a tight flame
of panic, an instantaneous
prison of fury as the sun
growled in the bell of heaven.

In electric passage through
the blood alarm split
adrenaline into crystal
that fixed in rigid balance

the planes and spirals of your
body. There is a fish
that in the chase of the shark
inflates itself into a ball

and crowds fin, scale and skeleton
into a ridge of coral. In
a slow burn of frenzy
on the scaffold of a hot Sunday

you fell in a fiery relief
and turned your clamor on
terraces of muscle and reposed—
the perfect sinew of fury.

A Movement of Peoples

Under the bulb the stun
of rain grinds flowers
out of stone, flame
from marble roots.

Widows, hunters, men
with their sons' singing
in their hearts, climb
past falcons and fall

into the stars. Chaos
tears golden rings away,
silver snakes and opals
from the crusted thigh;

the pyramid, the true stone,
the lonesome king; roam
the Egyptian ladies
in the gardens of Tut.

A hand grieves music from
a river. (Likeliness of lotus
and aster, green stalk and
a white orient tree.)

The hippo stumbles and a force
of gathering wheels
flips the poles, the world dips
and stands inverted.

A Reflection on the Paraclete

This is Melchizedek's year. I have thoughts
of altars and watch the world like an eagle
drawing his beak on a climber's eye. I caught
the sublimely very beautiful and in my mind,
thrumming, came the paraclete, as in the cave
of Plato came the masquerading light.
The ridge of the delectable mountains
breaks the light and in the cattails and
clover of the Jordan stands the Great Blue Heron.

The Blood

The blood is everything,
all potentates, all oracles,
all dancing-men agree. Tigers
sauntering through the light
come to the land of body
to rejoice. In seasons of jonquil,
like a crown, high, touched for trumpet,
the blood, dark as a span of mask,
does antics in the noonday.

The Death of a Poor Man

The world is cold by nature. It thinks
of death but not of catafalques and
the heavy wreathed wagon. The soul
of a poor man like Jonah in a sea of whale,
dodging consummation, flashes among
the waters and calls out decretals
of brown bread, hosannas of milk,
and liturgies of beef. The poor man
carried desolation uncommanded by desire
but spellbound by survival he crossed
the lintel into the famous world.

I think of this poor man and his
imperial dream, who dreamed of the sun
flashing unhooded in his eyes, who
imagined heaven as an order of wench
and daisies of chocolate.

The cornflower burning at midsummer
turns the fisherman from the stream.
The river sizzles on the red-hot slate.
In a poor man consummation builds
its holocaust and from the earth comes
a laying on of hands and the instantaneous encounter.

The Days of the Creation of the World

I   GOD THINKS ABOUT HIMSELF

I have no measure
I have no weight
I am prince and kingdom of my estate.

I know no distance
I know no fear
I am field and sky and hemisphere.

I've carved no image
I've built no dam
I am rule and forge and artisan.

I am God
I am one
I've sphered the earth and moon and sun.

I am fire
I am air
I am earth and water, all things fair.

I ponder man
I reckon love
I am ark and laurel; eagle and dove.

II   GOD CREATES THE SUN

In the halt before the establishment
of light, love divided from its
immediate site and God's head glowed
like fire in a cage. And he beat
the drum of his brain
and saw the sun.

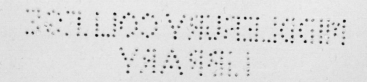

III GOD CREATES WATER

There had to be a way to show
that love freely given was the mark
of absolute simplicity; not one foot
after another on the way
to the temple, but without halter
like a horse in April
and God touched his side
and fashioned water.

IV GOD CREATES BIRDS

The journey from there to here
through the seizure of time
was a deed to be done
and the thought had need
of a sign. God heard
the spirit rock the dovecote
and craftily released the bird.

V GOD CREATES ADAM AND EVE

From the sod and the roots of trees,
from the sun's crystal and the salt's
tang, from rocks and the new waters,
from the air and the sand, God drew
his face upon the land and thought
himself from speculation into
form. From these lines Adam danced.
God watched him wake and gave him
Eve for goodness' sake.

Spring

Nunc Stuporem Meum Deus Rector Exaggerat.
—BOETHIUS

Now God, being my Governor, my astonishment
is increased. I take no long walk but his
compass draws me north, south, east, west
into the four seasons of his wit. The world
is his dominion, expert, bright and meta-
physical. In this assembly of days, my Rector
walks on the plains of intellect,
as the long fires on the sun's face draw
hot meridians on astronomer's glass.

Troubled by thoughts of deities, an Olympian
lady wished that God would come unhooded
to her room, but when God came he came as Fireman
and into cinders went that curious wench.
My Rector comes in the runes and spells of spring
when the dew falls low in the grass
and the morning-glory storms the garden wall.
In the zodiac of April, God, being my Governor,
falls in the mint and flowers of the sun.

The Summer

This is the sun's high exultation
and the ample months of the lark's
preference. Beasts roam without
dreams and there are keels in
the water and dragonflies cross
the air. Children catch
the phosphorescent fly and light
decreases. The Borealis and Zephyr
from the northern sea set off
explosions in the scalding air
and a curious passion, fixed
in the heart by nights of crazy
dreams, cuts the legs from under me
and in the passages of dark,
in the summer's long intensity,
the body learns the canons and conditions
of the heart. (O summer's not
for Manichees.) This is the manner
of the season and from sleep,
current with burning, I wake
to massing butterflies
and my son's hurrahs on the widowswalk.

The Ear in Autumn: An Instruction for the Wild Sara

This is the bellowing place
where the pumpkin sizzles
with sin and a strange wind
moves through the thickets
of the brain. On the top
of the sea waves' spines crack,
and the Sphinx appears
in the cornfield where the ample
witch sweeps across the eye.

Into the skull's bright auditorium,
into the celebrated labyrinth,
like Pierrot from balancing
broken on a parallel of light,
sound, manifest and real,
sets down its noise, hot
with the flames of late September.

It's Halloween, the time of the
apple bucket and the masked child.
Loud in the channels of the brain,
loud in the zodiac,
loud in the night, I hear
the rending of seasons,
and the ice-flow moves like a mast
through the heart.

Winter

In oblique stilettos the winter sun
falls in the plazas and gardens.
The red berry, a scarlet bullet,
hardens on the vine. The beaver
dams the river called the winterbourne
and the hawk glides like a skater
on a storm of freezing air. Noonday flowers:
the wall cracks and roots of chill
trace hexagons on the windowpanes
as if honeycombs were there the summer long.

The matter of intellect is arctic.
                                 Hidden
with the clatter of ice and too many freezings
it builds an arena of glazed sound in the ear:
the lean bitter season. Words come slowly
from the throat as if the chords and keys
of the heart forded the space of thought
blind as hunters lost on the polar cap.
Eyes and fingers blink in the sun, the hat
is brought down over the ears and the reign
of intellect collapses on petrified oceans of snow.

The Hunter

I heard you did a feat with a bull
and know Jehovah. You think of God
and love the hunt, exult in the designs
of plenty, the partridge and the deer
who stride like towers
through the night. You drop
the hedgehog from the branch
and the bear falls formally to the ground
in a hot blizzard. The world holds
the hunter and the priest,
the seal's glass pelt,
the bull in the field, the taurine broil,
this kingdom's multiple arks of animal.

Soon after Pentecost when the oils
were singing in the clay pots
and the fire of fire stepped
on your tongue, when the thistle
in cocky purple and the spring daisy
grew in trenches of boiling frost,
you grappled with the bull
of all disaster and bent its head
to the ground.
The errant priest set foot upon
his trophy in the sun
as a commander of armies
in the presence of the king holds up
his standard bright in the summary of exploit.

29

Adam's Hymn to His Body

I have high hopes for passion;
for I was once initiate there
and did high jinks in the fashion
of lovers: the hot jig on her bare
belly. My green spine
flowered; a branch broke
through my thigh, time
roistered and sweetly stroked
my brain and fired
the clay in my groin; we grieved;
clay expired
and Omega conceived

the exactions of Adam.
Now after long tournaments
in the arenas of madmen
I've made a pact with glory; torrents
of size and depth rile
on my eyes; falcons in jackets
of mail pace the file
of hunters in my thigh; rackets
of locust and honey bee
bolt on my lips; I've moved
down the face of the sun; the sea
mounts my eyes; I've proved

my body and stand in the light
of spring on the quick earth
where crocus and the night
beasts cut through the dirt
and cataracts of wind drill
like beetles in the shade.
The fields are densities of stone; the kill
of the scythe and the rattler unbraid
this sweet machine
my body; my clock, my element.
O hovering face! O green
mysterium; O high imperial pediment.

Two Poems on Larger Topics

I

From the circle's almighty roundness
the fires from the hot worlds
like tumblers through burning hoops
set all perimeters askew and
unstopped the tincts and symbols
in my mind as the whale upturns
the whaler and the sea.

II

In the locked air
the mind moves;
like a moving cell
in the strait world,
fair as perfect wheat.

It is meet
that the rivers in the sun
and the hillocks
in clouds; that the closed
fathoms of the sea

contend to be
image and mandate
of their mindless quiet.
But the mind is called
to silence and pure

stillness. As the lure
of fire called Yahweh
to the bush, so
on the mind's curve
light falls

and calls
rivers from the sun
and vineyards from the clouds.
In the locked air
the mind moves

toward its unutterable quiet.

A Homage to My Jewish Students at Christmas Time

In New England, a quiet place
with no extravagance of race
to hallow it, I tended toward
manner and repose, went schooling
in an ancient house and dreamed
of deer and crocuses. (Noah
would have left me in the rain
for I confused my sweetness
with my blood and thought the deer
lovelier than the mind.)

Guarded by the lion on our silver
crest I stalked through fields of lilies
in a sable sun to find my fantasies'
repose. (Though once I heard
that Moses drew fresh water from
a rock and thought that men of such
intent must be considerably divine.)

In our house God walked the ceilings
as a spider walks the undersides
of beams, or fire chimes out noon
on the sundial's face.
                        But you brought
God to me unspelled and reasoned
with my decorous intent and in this season
of Yahweh's stock I hear severing
Judith and the salts in my blood
build effigies and burning villages
and I think of the time God was on
mountains and division swam the sea.

Great Grandfather, Clam Diggers and Homer

I

His family was like Spaniards
on horses; like prophets
their heads; superb with ladies;
bodies like cherry wood;
necks like chalices and eyes
that caught light as the sea
holds the sun; hunters who dreamed
the malediction of the fox.

But his youngest son, as the ellipse
describes the wave, in the skills
of discontent, drew masts down
the margins of books, calipered hulls
on his bedroom walls, for Poseidon
(rumored in tempests) laid his trident
like wings upon his eyes.

II

Though his father had no passion
for the sea, he built his son a boat
in the image of the one Odysseus
took to get away from Troy
and one day when a strong west wind
had touched the sound, his boy,
stripped to the sun and the oar's tug,
piloted that barge down the channel
to the sea and in Greek, pure
as the air that touches snow
(the sun of Asia glowed in the noise),
he read of the voyage through
the Dardanelles, past Sunium and Corinth
down the currents to Ithaca where sunrise
and hot temples rose in the burning
noon and the household waited
like traps in the timbered hall.

III

The clam diggers laughed: "What's this,
pressing through the morning?" "What noise,
what conspiracy? O Watch."

IV

At noonday, with bells and gulls
and white sail, a boy, arms red
with the hot light, and an old man
singing glided to the bottom
of the dock where a groom pulled
with ropes grecian music to a standstill.

Penelope, a flower, raised
her parasol and beckoned to the singer
to come up the stairway from the sea
into the blue air where a carriage
waited and a chestnut mare.

The boy who rowed the singer through
the waves, the salt air like a net
of marble on his back, laid his head upon
the oarlocks and dreamed of the light
on waves and Poseidon enthroned.

Two Poems on the Creation of a Statue of a Maenad

I   THE MAENAD TO ALDO JOHN CASANOVA

I am freewheeling. The unslung hoop
in my blood tingles at nightfall.
Through the briar and onion beds;
through the sacred rivers, up the rocky air,
in the white hazards of the moon,
scooping pebbles for my catapult
I wolf the night.

There is the process of metal in me;
the hardening of the light that gives
the lucent glory to the eye . . .
the dark clatter of gears and the mechanical
clicks of the tissue of fury.
I've watched Dionysus step like a scimitar
through my side.

I know the face of fire on fire.
I've chewed the neck of lambs,
devoured the hare, brought the hot
pyre of my nails to the wolf's eyes,
rooted into the backs of deer with
my toes and shattered quail
with my fist.

I am freewheeling
and follow my blood wherever it goes.
As some men follow fire, others their nose.

II   ALDO JOHN CASANOVA TO THE MAENAD

In my studio I have built a stand
where I set out a bunch of iron
sticks and clamps to fasten down
the Maenad in my mind. In the focus
of my inner eye, like an apple or
a crystal on a shelf, I reckon
where a Maenad's spine should be
and how the implications in her neck
would suffer under fire.

I drove her into place with double
clamps; arms, legs, hips, thigh,
groin; the raving brow, the vulture
lips; a frame of steel to hold
her skeleton intact for she had shifted
her position once and in my mind
an unsettling took place and the clamps
pulled from the wood and the frame
of steel unfastened in my hands.

It is not easy for a Maenad to keep
still. The rip-tides and bandits
in her blood will not pose upon
a pedestal. But when I clamp down
this first double cord of steel
and set her feet upon a soldered place
she'll rouse the anvil and the furnace
in my arms and I'll predict in steel
and flame the lineaments of bacchanalia.

An Afternoon with a Poet

There where transported, partial Greece
is horticulture to a Gallic weed,
music flung from a balcony, wrought
with iron leaves, the poet drawled
his preference, his Saint,
the phrase before the husband strophe.
The cultured lady in abject understanding
sits near a torso of Alexander and knits
her pencil to his mimicry.

What do you think about? In other words
Who are you?
                (I am the custom of my set
                the archangel who is tribal lore.)

Will the wheat come brown and cold?
                (The wheat grows in my beloved's hand
                and it grows brown and cold.)

Do you really see color in a rhino's tusk
Is the rabbit triangular in the corpulent
hunter's bow?
                (When the horn flares up and flute
                boondaggles you, you'll know whose
                song it is.)

Into the seer's dark afternoon she
froze him and his book into her eye—
river of hand resting like a roundelay
upon his cheek, eyes reaching with attendant
birds along the path of music to behold
behold, behold the belovely face—
the charming sinless head . . .

The Poet as Stutterer

He is a very lame duck
on a branch, watching the
luck of the shooter
marching in the rushes,
while going on within
remains; the harvest,
the rough divinity,
listening to the rage
of the partridge come upon.
But better not to scorn
though lip hooks thorn,
laminates: qualities there
under the double phonic.
Like a garland on a dark animal
he strides Alphabet.
Like a guilty dwarf
who sees a smaller brother
he goes to pieces at a word,
for when meeting "B" the rest fall
unremittingly to his combustion.

                                    Then
horn flared and flute boondaggled.
And immensely grave a silver clown
toweled in a cape transfigured
with peacock and ibis eyes
yawned and lifted up his perfect arms,
consumed the sun and fled into the dark.
Then he who spoke to the solitary heart
floated up a burning stair and vanished
wordless and omnipotent to Variegation
and burnished Pierrot.

Certain Reflections on What I Saw

In the precision of fear
I have observed these things
for there is no mood or passion
called forth from the extravagance
of memory and the spirit's
underworld that does not pass through
the blood, untried in the fires
of the eye:

The ape in the tower of his rage;
two children severing a barge
from the rope that holds it from
the sea; the arctic in white
meridians and mountains blue
in the salt air;
the flying fish aprowl for light
that falls through fathoms;
the high priest in his mask
rising in the dark like a knife
to unclasp the stag
from the polar brush.

From these things I conclude
this logic:

The ape is the possessor of rage
and with it is terrible;
children sunder and the arctic
is the cold land of universe
where we watch for light
and the glacier's stutter;
the priest is Adam alchemical
who'd transform all mud
to archangel.

And from the intolerable waters
up leaps Ichthus the flying fish
cracking the waves in lunacy
to meet the transforming sun.

Through the Steel Haze

Through the steel haze
the bride walks and the sea
is high with stamping
horses.
  The blue of their
eyes bores through the light
and passion is brought to a high
burn.
  O Thalassio.
Bricks crack through the
lion's pelt and the animal
paces the gazelle through
the afternoon.

The sun falls on her hair
and her arms shoot into
the air swinging in a circle
a lasso of marvelous hemp

brought from the extremes
of Asia.
  In the bed of the sea
coral snaps from the sea walls
and one by one the hinges fall
from the locks of the great canals
in the valleys of the world's
center.
  In the boon of glory,
with all her people shouting
in her wake, the bride walks
through the steel haze
drawn by harrowing winds
and the bridegroom's hurrah
to the tumultuous chamber.

Ventus increbrescit.
O Thalassio.

Two Poems on Aspects of Light

I

From the hands she traced numbers with
fidgets a light, a light on a tree,
tree in the morning, morning tree.
In the end of flame, when
heat has the tenderness of rivers,
fire burns form from prosaic clay.
Lux is the shape, lux is tenebrae,
in a tingling circuit round the sun.

II

Drawn by the focus, in a delicate line
the light of day reels through the mind
drawn by the shaped climacteric of
the sun. Light fantastically prepares
the limited alphabet. Adam to his
Hecuba growls in the sun.

Speak This Slowly

I

Speak this slowly as the sound of stone,
in earth-covered company
with the head bent in darkness.
Render this song to the dark crowd.
Rest the head gently, make hidden the eye.
Render this song to the dark crowd.

Fathoms down the loon laughs straight
in the face of spangled fish, the
coral lurks in the light, a sea music.
In the corner of the valley beneath
an oak, Corinna works a deception.
Shepherds come upon a tomb, the valley
lurks, an earth sound comes from the air.

II

The scratched face of Corinna leans
over the pastoral acre.
She gives her ballad to the animals in cover.

Come down to the valley, loon in the sea,
break every stone, let loon-laughter free
all the lost possibilities, all the vanished army.

The loon flies high
and the trees in the meadow
reach up, hearing the sound of wing and
the hilarity of the fowl.

Falstaff

O thou indiscreet Hamlet of the bush
watched by the cockerel in the coop
hot in the night of the north winds.

Thy heart is a doxy with a clipper-
shaped jaw, full of timbre and jog

which services the patched-up wench
who will sell her dishes for love
her goat for your beating
is charm to the jinxed bull of the world

fumbling with the young shoulder, while
you plant a hanker in the chaste swan.

(Somewhere, untwirled, the moor
drags his golden turban on the floor;
a daughter-dragged king makes
crowns from eternal daisies.)

Up with you, up from your sleeping
up to the cliff where the sun fell,
where a Druid girl left her body
printed in lime, fallen in an ancient frost.

Up with you now, Thou Crest, Thou Rooster,
Thou Haphazard, Thou Bug, Thou Plaything.

The Tent, the Song, the Sign, the Element

I THE TENT

In God's tent the sun,
God walks and carpets
and braziers are set out
on his frying lawn where
poles and pulleys,
rings and intersecting
ropes, various nails
and locking joints spend away
in a hot pavilion
where God turns about
and then about again and
stands his ground like a tower
of smoke and bends back
his head and through
the hole in the top of his red-hot tent
two winged bolts of fire rocket from his eyes
and fly red and full of sparks
as if they were bright hackle on a line
toward the depths of the sea,
bait for the blue, the fan-tailed shark.

II THE SONG

Cut said the owl, cut down the night
Crack said the fawn, crack down the hunter
Lash said the ermine, lash up the owl
Plant said the snake, plant down the hunter
Row said the sailor, row through the night
Blow said the trumpet, blow away the sailor
Pierce said the arrow, pierce through the trumpeter
Leap said the hoop, leap through the archer
Strike said the firebrand, strike down the fawn
Torch said the hunter, torch to the sailor
Sun said the owl, sun on the owl's eyes
Rain said the farmer, rain on the wheatfields
And I rode on the lip of the trumpet in the coop of the sun.

III   THE SIGN

I have brought intense darkness
to light, so stone that it knocked
down fences. I have brought pure thought
from multicolored valleys.
I have touched the sides of mountains
that would have leapt had I commanded
them to leap. The Foscalano would have
leapt and all the animals in Abruzzi
but I commanded only words and the air
bridled like a stallion at the tug
of my hands and to the far and pitchest
fathoms I brought the praise of light
sidesaddle on the sun.

IV   THE ELEMENT

At the nub of radium
at the hollow of the atom
where space is fixed upon
a point of black light,
a jut of green casts into
the beating element
at the nub of radium
seething with dyes and coils
of ether, pointed like stakes,
there at the peak of the atom
where I planted a flag and drew upon my map
the river and the shepherd
one coursing on the ice of the valley
the other leaping a chasm
his crook slashing the air like a scimitar.
I set my blazon in the snow
at this height, at the nub of radium,
where the pennon hums and flashes in a blast of suns.

The Boyhood of Nguyen Van Vinh

My boyhood had an island,
a grayhound, and a white tree,
two birds, a regnant witch,
a pirate and a mystery.

This island had a mountain
with a cave and a craven shrine;
the sun was a mesozoic plant
and the sea was a roaring vine.

This mountain had a nether side,
a dark kingdom and a cliff;
an alert tiger, a sharp rain,
an alphabet and a blue skiff.

I sang high songs of pilgrims
and watched the marvelous light,
as the tiger flexed his ripping paws
and eagles scratched the night.

My island had a den of winds
and a black stag in a walled park.
I dreamed the arts of malcontent
and dwelled in the zones of dark.

But came a day, a fractured time
when in the alleys of the hill
explosions, comets, feats of suns
took brute occasion of my will
and since I feared that I might die
I raised the spritsail in the rain
and turned my blue skiff through the dark
as birds in a white tree shook my brain.

43
To X

You said: I had a dream of beauty
and in a disposition pricked
with hummingbirds and shells,
I brought a girl down on my bed
and held her in the naked mirror
of my hands.
           She had no place upon
that open scene, standing
in a torrid shade. The sun faced
her head with a high screen
of thought and the hills touched
the brim of my mind
where white trees burned
in the brine.
           The cold ship
of my heart swerved on a new tangent,
tacked perpendicular and the tempest within
raised the blood high on a brazen shelf.

I heard a cry of windows;
the grain reversed in the oak door,
the walls cleaved open and the ceiling fell
upon the floor. The house pulled
at my eyes and the stairway rung
with crowds.
           (We walked past Casa d'Oro
and when I pointed out the glittering
balustrade you said you could not see it
for you wept.)
I saw my mother straddling the doorsill
bent over in a hoop of chill
and when the wainscot pushed aside the beams
and the bedposts crackled in points of fire
I felt my brain constrict and fell upon the floor
and two coiled hands applauded at the door.

Johanna, the Big Cow

Heu! Johanna is the big cow
looming with milk over
the pen gate and like disciples
on a visionary hike
we move in upon that citadel
of hay and lead her wobbling
toward the stanchions
in the middle of the earth and
bring down boiling into bright steel pails
incredible quarts of milk.
No wonder the barn steams with our breathing
and our thighs bucking Johanna
tingle with the calories of winter.

High to the knees in dung
the eyes braised with cold winds
our spines rock
like rods of iron
in a heaving wall.
Johanna stands intact
as the tug of the electric cups
draws out her white honey
her blanch ichor
into bright steel pails.

Heu! What passion in stanchions,
what procession in cows coming down the road
to be milked.
I cannot remember such high prancing
though once I watched the horses
of a mortal king step into a tent
on a visionary progress
and shake their manes in the sun.

The Beginning of Jewels

EMERALD

The grasses, on a sudden, tormented
by whistling boys and golden heads
fell into the earth and grappled
a crystal seed and were hammered
in the sun's hammering to emerald.

PEARL

When the Oyster drew in upon itself
and noted its elect condition
it traced a perfect circle,
shelled, aquatic, white . . .
and at the center, on a point
of sand, it focused its attention.

RUBY

I think that if darkness
at its blackest, at the
limit of exclusion, at the
cornering of antipodes when the poles
arch against light . . . if then,
at the farthest boundary
at the level of waters where
light is turned back into the air,
if then, dark exploded as a vein
explodes on the heart,
from the dusky currents and ribs
of pitch there would be
a beginning of rubies.

SAPPHIRE

On the face of mica and slate
there is a geologic blue balance
and marks of birds that drew
the points of their flight across
the sky like nets. On the edge
of the planes, on the molten axis
of rock a fire crackles, and
as it feeds inward to consume the center
sapphire mounts spirals of crystal.

46

Webbed, Yellow-Billed and Aquamarine

Webbed, yellow-billed and aquamarine
he was born early to a world of no ducks.
He barked under the willow in the studded air
of bitter flies and nested in the sun.
His companions were dogs; no other duck
he ever knew but himself which conversed
with dogs, learned dogs and followed dogs
throughout the day, though rightly duck
was canine in rhetoric. Nature saw duck
and judged it plumed; this animal knew himself
dog and flew at cats and awaited at the gate
his master's coming. (Though once in the shade
of a flowering window he wished he could tell
the tale of the day he was a swan and encountered
a lady lying on the banks of a wild and singing river.)

To Brother Joseph of Mount Savior

I have encountered the radical man,
who is courteous and praises God
all day. I have seen in him no lapsed
thought, no averted watch and he walks
with the long strides of great men.
I saw him work in a ritual of sinew
among bales of hay where in the pollen
and fahrenheit of June he made antiphons
out of timothy. (Titian would have
painted him in a linen ruff on a golden
chair.) Mastered splendidly by God
in the superior labor of praise
he moved with the gentleness of waters
and the extravagance of lions.

The Death of a Racing-Car Driver

Boom and then the wind deliberated where
to blow his body. The woodbine urged
it come and startle moles from breakfasting
on woodbine, moles connived to make it
Palace for the King of Moles and roots
dismayed with dark cried, "Turn to light
and fire all these caves of underground."

The argument continued through the night.
Where to put him? Now he had no say,
no shaft to mark the way, no unity—broken
short the point of sundering, a diamond
delivered up to coronets and bishops' staffs.
He lay amid the courts of funeral, a genial prize,
severed in two; a duplicate disaster

and would not meet again except
as trickery in some mortician's shop. At dawn
the parliaments divided up the loot
and pondered the duration of their world.
The woodbine heard an exodus of moles and
coronations' hot regalia stumbled through
a temple joined with pistons, bolts and pipe.

And when mothers found their way to envelopes
of hair and widows brought out veils from
bridal chests, the racer's body, tarnished
in the sun, found condition in the trembling
earth and rested there with pollen on his lips
waiting for the horns that lay like crickets
in the fields of May.

DATE DUE

DATE DUE		
5/9/08		